C000041104

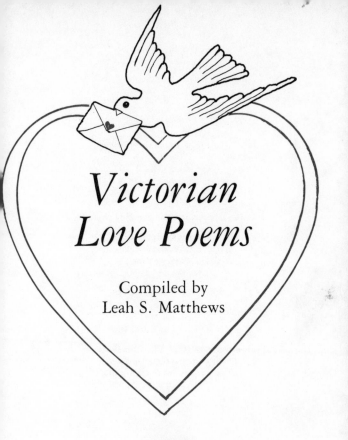

Victorian Love Poems

Compiled by
Leah S. Matthews

PIATKUS

© 1987 by Judy Piatkus (Publishers) Ltd

First published in Great Britain
in 1987 by
Judy Piatkus (Publishers) Ltd
5 Windmill Street, London W1P 1HF

British Library Cataloguing in Publication Data

Victorian love poems.
1. Love poetry, English
I. Matthews, Leah S.
821'008'0354   PR1184

ISBN 0–86188–655–0

Cover designed and
illustrated by Joanna Isles

Phototypeset in 10/11pt Linotron Garamond by
Phoenix Photosetting, Chatham, Kent
Printed and bound in Great Britain at
The Bath Press, Bath

Contents

Meeting

DORA GREENWELL
A Picture

It was in autumn that I met
  Her whom I love; the sunflowers bold
Stood up like guards around her set,
And all the air with mignonette
  Was warm within the garden old;
  Beside her feet the marigold
Glowed star-like, and the sweet-pea sent
A sigh to follow as she went
Slowly adown the terrace; – there
I saw thee, oh my love! and thou wert fair.

She stood in the full noonday, unafraid,
  As one beloved of sunlight, for awhile
She leant upon the timeworn balustrade;
The white clematis wooed her, and the clove
  Hung all its burning heart upon her smile;
And on her cheek and in her eyes was love;
And on her lips that, like an opening rose,
Seemed parting some sweet secret to disclose,
The soul of all the summer lingered; – there
I saw thee, oh my love! and thou wert fair.

CHRISTINA ROSSETTI
The First Day

I wish I could remember the first day,
First hour, first moment of your meeting me;
If bright or dim the season, it might be
Summer or winter for aught I can say.
So unrecorded did it slip away,
So blind was I to see and foresee,
So dull to mark the budding of my tree
That would not blossom yet for many a May.

If only I could recollect it! Such
A day of days! I let it come and go
As traceless as a thaw of bygone snow.
It seemed to mean so little, meant so much!
If only now I could recall that touch,
First touch of hand in hand! – Did one but know!

WILLIAM HURRELL MALLOCK
Brussels and Oxford

How first we met do you still remember?
 Do you still remember our last adieu?
You were all to me, that sweet September:
 Oh, what, I wonder, was I to you?

But I will not ask. I will leave in haze
 My thoughts of you, and your thoughts of me;
And will rest content that those sweet fleet days
 Are still my tenderest memory.

I often dream how we went together
 Mid glimmering leaves and glittering lights,
And watched the twilight Belgian weather
 Dying into the starriest nights;

And over our heads the throbbing million
 Of bright fires beat, like my heart, on high;
And the music clashed from the lit pavilion,
 And we were together, you and I.

But a hollow memory now suffices
 For what, last summer, was real and true;
Since here I am by the misty Isis,
 And under the fogs of London you.

But what if you, like a swift magician,
    Were to change the failing, flowerless year –
Were to make that true that is now a vision,
    And to bring back summer and Brussels here?

For Fanny, I know, that if you come hither
    You will bring with you the time of flowers,
And a breath of the tender Belgian weather,
    To Oxford's grey autumnal towers.

And in frost and fog though the late year dies,
    Yet the hours again will be warm and fair,
If they meet once more in your dark, deep eyes,
    And are meshed again in your golden hair.

THOMAS BURBIDGE
She Bewitched Me

She bewitched me
With such a sweet and genial charm,
I knew not when I wounded was,
And when I found it, hugged the harm.

Down hill, ah yes – down hill, down hill I glide,
But such a hill!
One tapestried fall of meadow pride,
Of ladysmock and daffodil.

How soon, how soon adown a rocky stair,
And slips no longer smooth as they are sweet,
Shall I, with backward-streaming hair,
Outfly my bleeding feet?

AUSTIN DOBSON
Incognita

Just for a space that I met her –
    Just for a day in the train!
It began when she feared it would wet her,
    That tiniest spurtle of rain:
So we tucked a great rug in the sashes,
    And carefully padded the pane;
And I sorrow in sackcloth and ashes,
    Longing to do it again!

Then it grew when she begged me to reach her
    A dressing-case under the seat;
She was 'really so tiny a creature,
    That she needed a stool for her feet!'
Which was promptly arranged to her order
    With a care that was even minute,
And a glimpse – of an open-worked border,
    And a glance – of the fairyest boot.

Then it drooped, and revived at some hovels –
    'Were they houses for men or for pigs?'
Then it shifted to muscular novels,
    With a little digression on prigs:
She thought 'Wives and Daughters' '*so* jolly';
    'Had I read it?' She knew when I had,
Like the rest, I should dote upon 'Molly';
    And 'poor Mrs Gaskell – how sad!'

'Like Browning?' 'But so-so.' His proof lay
    Too deep for her frivolous mood,
That preferred your mere metrical *soufflé*
    To the stronger poetical food;
Yet at times he was good – 'as a tonic';
    Was Tennyson writing just now?
And was this new poet Byronic,
    And clever, and naughty, or how?

Then we trifled with concerts and croquet,
    Then she daintily dusted her face;
Then she sprinkled herself with 'Ess Bouquet',
    Fished out from the foregoing case;
And we chattered of Gassier and Grisi,
    And voted Aunt Sally a bore;
Discussed if the tight rope were easy,
    Or Chopin much harder than Spohr.

And oh! the odd things that she quoted,
    With the prettiest possible look,
And the price of two buns that she noted
    In the prettiest possible book;
While her talk like a musical rillet
    Flashed on with the hours that flew,
And the carriage, her smile seemed to fill it
    With just enough summer – for Two.

Till at last in her corner, peeping
    From a nest of rugs and of furs,
With the white shut eyelids sleeping
    On those dangerous looks of hers,
She seemed like a snowdrop breaking,
    Not wholly alive nor dead,
But with one blind impulse making
    To the sounds of the spring overhead;

And I watched in the lamplight's swerving
    The shade of the down-dropped lid,
And the lip-line's delicate curving,
    Where a slumbering smile lay hid,
'Till I longed that, rather than sever,
    The train should shriek into space,
And carry us onward – for ever –
    Me and that beautiful face.

But she suddenly woke in a fidget,
    With fears she was 'nearly at home',
And talk of a certain Aunt Bridget,
    Whom I mentally wished – well at Rome;
Got out at the very next station,
    Looking back with a merry *Bon Soir*,
Adding, too, to my utter vexation,
    A surplus, unkind *Au Revoir*.

So left me to muse on her graces,
    To doze and to muse, till I dreamed
That we sailed through the sunniest places
    In a glorified galley, it seemed;
But the cabin was made of a carriage,
    And the ocean was Eau-de-Cologne,
And we split on a rock labelled MARRIAGE,
    And I woke, – as cold as a stone.

And that's how I lost her – a jewel,
    Incognita – one in a crowd,
Not prudent enough to be cruel,
    Not worldly enough to be proud.
It was just a shut lid and its lashes,
    Just a few hours in a train,
And I sorrow in sackcloth and ashes,
    Longing to see her again.

THOMAS HARDY

A Thunderstorm in Town
(A Reminiscence: 1893)

She wore a new 'terra-cotta' dress,
And we stayed, because of the pelting storm,
Within the hansom's dry recess,
Though the horse had stopped; yea, motionless
   We sat on, snug and warm.

Then the downpour ceased, to my sharp sad pain
And the glass that had screened our forms before
Flew up, and out she sprang to her door:
I should have kissed her if the rain
   Had lasted a minute more.

Lady Jingly answered sadly,
    And her tears began to flow,—
        'Your proposal comes too late,
    Mr. Yonghy-Bonghy-Bo!
I would be your wife most gladly!'
(Here she twirled her fingers madly)
        'But in England I've a mate!
        Yes! you've asked me far too late,
        For in England I've a mate,
    Mr. Yonghy-Bonghy-Bo!
    Mr. Yonghy-Bonghy-Bo!

'Mr. Jones — (his name is Handel,—
    Handel Jones, Esquire, & Co.)
        Dorking fowls delights to send,—
    Mr. Yonghy-Bonghy-Bo!
Keep, oh! keep your chairs and candle,—
And your jug without a handle,—
        I can merely be your friend!
        — Should my Jones more Dorkings send,
        I will give you three, my friend!
    Mr. Yonghy-Bonghy-Bo!
    Mr. Yonghy-Bonghy-Bo!

'Though you've such a tiny body,
  And your head so large doth grow,—
    Though your hat may blow away,
  Mr. Yonghy-Bonghy-Bo!
Though you're such a Hoddy Doddy —
Yet I wish that I could modi-
    fy the words I needs must say!
    Will you please to go away?
    That is all I have to say —
  Mr. Yonghy-Bonghy-Bo!
  Mr. Yonghy-Bonghy-Bo!'

Down the slippery slopes of Myrtle,
  Where the early pumpkins blow,
    To the calm and silent sea
  Fled the Yonghy-Bonghy-Bo.
There, beyond the Bay of Gurtle,
Lay a large and lively Turtle;—
    'You're the Cove', he said, 'for me;
    On your back beyond the sea,
    Turtle, you shall carry me!'
  Said the Yonghy-Bonghy-Bo.
  Said the Yonghy-Bonghy-Bo.

Through the silent-roaring ocean
   Did the Turtle swiftly go;
      Holding fast upon his shell
   Rode the Yonghy-Bonghy-Bo.
With a sad primaeval motion
Towards the sunset isles of Boshen
      Still the Turtle bore him well.
      Holding fast upon his shell,
      'Lady Jingly Jones, farewell!'
   Sang the Yonghy-Bonghy-Bo.
   Sang the Yonghy-Bonghy-Bo.

From the Coast of Coromandel,
   Did the Lady never go;
      On the heap of stones she mourns
   For the Yonghy-Bonghy-Bo.
On the Coast of Coromandel,
In his jug without a handle,
      Still she weeps, and daily moans;
      On that little heap of stones
      To her Dorking Hens she moans,
   For the Yonghy-Bonghy-Bo.
   For the Yonghy-Bonghy-Bo.

Loving

ROBERT BROWNING

Never the Time and the Place

Never the time and the place
   And the loved one all together!
This path – how soft to pace!
   This May – what magic weather!
Where is the loved one's face?
In a dream that loved one's face meets mine,
   But the house is narrow, the place is bleak
Where, outside, rain and wind combine
   With a furtive ear, if I strive to speak,
   With hostile eye at my flushing cheek,
With a malice that marks each word, each sign!
O enemy sly and serpentine
   Uncoil thee from the waking man!
     Do I hold the Past
     Thus firm and fast
   Yet doubt if the Future hold I can
This path so soft to pace shall lead,
Thro' the magic of May to herself indeed!
Or narrow if needs the house must be,
Outside are the storms and strangers: we –
Oh, close, safe, warm sleep I and she,
– I and she!

JOHN CLARE

Mary

It is the evening hour,
   How silent all doth lie:
The hornèd moon she shows her face
   In the river with the sky.
Prest by the path on which we pass,
The flaggy lake lies still as glass.

Spirit of her I love,
   Whispering to me
Stores of sweet visions as I rove,
   Here stop, and crop with me
Sweet flowers that in the still hour grew –
We'll take them home, nor shake off the bright dew.

Mary, or sweet spirit of thee,
   As the bright sun shines to-morrow
Thy dark eyes these flowers shall see,
   Gathered by me in sorrow,
In the still hour when my mind was free
To walk alone – yet wish I walked with thee.

THOMAS MOORE
Did Not

'Twas a new feeling – something more
Than we had dared to own before,
    Which then we hid not;
We saw it in each other's eye,
And wished, in every half-breathed sigh,
    To speak, but did not.

She felt my lips' impassioned touch –
'Twas the first time I dared so much,
    And yet she chid not;
But whispered o'er my burning brow,
'Oh, do you doubt I love you now?'
    Sweet soul! I did not.

Warmly I felt her bosom thrill,
I pressed it closer, closer still,
    Though gently bid not;
Till – oh! the world hath seldom heard
Of lovers, who so nearly erred,
    And yet, who did not.

WATHEN MARK WILKS CALL

Summer Days

In summer, when the days were long,
We walked, two friends, in field and wood,
Our heart was light, our step was strong,
And life lay round us, fair as good,
In summer, when the days were long.

We strayed from morn till evening came,
We gathered flowers, and wove us crowns,
We walked mid poppies red as flame,
Or sat upon the yellow downs,
And always wished our life the same.

In summer, when the days were long,
We leapt the hedgerow, crossed the brook;
And still her voice flowed forth in song,
Or else she read some graceful book,
In summer, when the days were long.

And then we sat beneath the trees,
With shadows lessening in the noon;
And in the sunlight and the breeze,
We revelled, many a glorious June,
While larks were singing o'er the leas.

In summer, when the days were long,
We plucked wild strawberries, ripe and red,
Or feasted, with no grace but song,
On golden nectar, snow-white bread,
In summer, when the days were long.

We loved, and yet we knew it not,
For loving seemed like breathing then,
We found a heaven in every spot,
Saw angels, too, in all good men,
And dreamt of gods in grove and grot.

In summer, when the days are long,
Alone I wander, muse alone;
I see her not, but that old song,
Under the fragrant wind is blown,
In summer, when the days are long.

Alone I wander in the wood,
But one fair spirit hears my sighs;
And half I see the crimson hood,
The radiant hair, the calm glad eyes,
That charmed me in life's summer mood.

In summer, when the days are long,
I love her as I loved of old;
My heart is light, my step is strong,
For love brings back those hours of gold,
In summer, when the days are long.

DANTE GABRIEL ROSSETTI
Sudden Light

I have been here before,
    But when or how I cannot tell:
I know the grass beyond the door,
    The sweet keen smell,
The sighing sound, the lights around the shore.

You have been mine before,—
    How long ago I may not know:
But just when at that swallow's soar
    Your neck turned so,
Some veil did fall, — I knew it all of yore.

Has this been thus before?
    And shall not thus time's eddying flight
Still with our lives our love restore
    In death's despite,
And day and night yield one delight once more?

ALGERNON CHARLES SWINBURNE

Love and Sleep

Lying asleep between the strokes of night
   I saw my love lean over my sad bed,
   Pale as the duskiest lily's leaf or head,
Smooth-skinned and dark, with bare throat made to bite,
Too wan for blushing and too warm for white,
   But perfect-coloured without white or red.
And her lips opened amorously, and said –
I wist not what, saving one word – Delight.

And all her face was honey to my mouth,
   And all her body pasture to mine eyes;
      The long lithe arms and hotter hands than fire,
The quivering flanks, hair smelling of the south,
   The bright light feet, the splendid supple thighs
      And glittering eyelids of my soul's desire.

EDGAR ALLAN POE
To Helen

Helen, thy beauty is to me
  Like those Nicean barks of yore,
That gently o'er a perfumed sea,
  The weary, way-worn wanderer bore
  To his own native shore.

On desperate seas long wont to roam,
  Thy hyacinth hair, thy classic face,
Thy Naiad airs have brought me home
  To the glory that was Greece,
  And the grandeur that was Rome.

Lo! in yon brilliant window-niche
  How statue-like I see thee stand,
The agate lamp within thy hand!
  Ah, Psyche, from the regions which
  Are Holy-Land!

COVENTRY PATMORE
Love Serviceable

What measure Fate to him shall mete
   Is not the noble Lover's care;
He's heart-sick with a longing sweet
   To make her happy as she's fair.
Oh, misery should she him refuse,
   And so her dearest good mistake!
His own success he thus pursues
   With frantic zeal for her sole sake.

To lose her were his life to blight,
   Being loss to hers; to make her his,
Except as helping her delight,
   He calls but incidental bliss;
And, holding life as so much pelf
   To buy her posies, learns this lore:
He does not rightly love himself
   Who does not love another more.

ELIZABETH BARRETT BROWNING
From *Sonnets from the Portuguese*

XLIV

Belovèd, thou has brought me many flowers
Plucked in the garden, all the summer through
And winter, and it seemed as if they grew
In this close room, nor missed the sun and showers.
So, in the like name of that love of ours,
Take back these thoughts which here unfolded too,
And which on warm and cold days I withdrew
From my heart's ground. Indeed, those beds and bowers
Be overgrown with bitter weeds and rue,
And wait thy weeding; yet here's eglantine,
Here's ivy! – take them, as I used to do
Thy flowers, and keep them where they shall not pine.
Instruct thine eyes to keep their colours true,
And tell thy soul their roots are left in mine.

CHRISTINA WALSH

A Woman to Her Lover

(*'Proudly'*)

Do you come to me to bend me to your will
As conqueror to the vanquished
To make of me a bondslave
To bear you children, wearing out my life
In drudgery and silence
No servant will I be
If that be what you ask, O Lover (*'ironically'*) I refuse you!

(*'Mockingly-drawing room ballad style'*)

Or if you think to wed with one from heaven sent
Whose every deed and word and wish is golden
A wingless angel who can do no wrong
Go! – I am no doll to dress and sit for feeble worship
If that be what you ask, fool, I refuse you!

(*'Slowly'*)

Or if you think in me to find
A creature who will have no greater joy
Than gratify your clamorous desire,
My skin soft only for your fond caresses
My body supple only for your sense delight,
Oh shame, and pity and abasement.
Not for you the hand of any wakened woman of our time.

(35)

But Lover, if you ask of me
That I shall be your comrade, friend, and mate,
To live and work, to love and die with you,
That so together we may know the purity and height
Of passion, and of joy and sorrow,
Then O husband, I am yours forever
And our co-equal love will make the stars to laugh with joy
And we shall have the music of the spheres for bridal march
And to its circling fugue pass on, hand holding hand
Until we reach the very heart of God.

COVENTRY PATMORE

The Kiss

'I saw you take his kiss!' ''Tis true.'
  'O, modesty!' ''Twas strictly kept:
He thought me asleep: at least I knew
  He thought I thought he thought I slept.'

COVENTRY PATMORE
The Revelation

An idle poet, here and there,
  Looks round him; but, for all the rest
The world, unfathomably fair,
  Is duller than a witling's jest.
Love wakes men, once a lifetime each;
  They lift their heavy lids, and look;
And, lo, what one sweet page can teach
  They read with joy, then shut the book.
And some give thanks, and some blaspheme,
  And most forget; but, either way,
That and the Child's unheeded dream
  Is all the light of all their day.

LIONEL JOHNSON
A Decadent's Lyric

Sometimes, in very joy of shame,
Our flesh becomes one living flame:
And she and I
Are no more separate, but the same.

Ardour and agony unite;
Desire, delirium, delight:
And I and she
Faint in the fierce and fevered night.

Her body music is: and ah,
The accords of lute and viola,
When she and I
Play on live limbs love's opera!

THOMAS MOORE
The Kiss

Give me, my love, that billing kiss
   I taught you one delicious night,
When, turning epicures in bliss,
   We tried inventions of delight.

Come, gently steal my lips along,
   And let your lips in murmurs move,–
Ah, no! – again – that kiss was wrong –
   How can you be so dull, my love?

'Cease, cease!' the blushing girl replied –
   And in her milky arms she caught me –
'How can you thus your pupil chide;
   You know *'twas in the dark* you taught me!'

ELIZABETH BARRETT BROWNING

From *Sonnets from the Portuguese*

XLIII

How do I love thee? Let me count the ways.
I love thee to the depth and breadth and height
My soul can reach, when feeling out of sight
For the ends of Being and ideal Grace.
I love thee to the level of everyday's
Most quiet need, by sun and candle-light.
I love thee freely, as men strive for Right;
I love thee purely, as they turn from Praise.
I love thee with the passion put to use
In my old griefs, and with my childhood's faith.
I love thee with a love I seemed to lose
With my lost saints, – I love thee with the breath,
Smiles, tears, of all my life! – and, if God choose,
I shall but love thee better after death.

CHARLES BAUDELAIRE
The Jewels

My well-beloved was stripped. Knowing my whim,
She wore her tinkling gems, but naught besides:
And showed such pride as, while her luck betides,
A sultan's favoured slave may show to him.

When it lets off its lively, crackling sound,
This blazing blend of metal crossed with stone,
Gives me an ecstasy I've only known
Where league of sound and lustre can be found.

She let herself be loved: then, drowsy-eyed,
Smiled down from her high couch in languid ease.
My love was deep and gentle as the seas
And rose to her as to a cliff the tide.

My own approval of each dreamy pose,
Like a tamed tiger, cunningly she sighted:
And candour, with lubricity united,
Gave piquancy to every one she chose.

Her limbs and hips, burnished with changing lustres,
Before my eyes clairvoyant and serene,
Swanned themselves, undulating in their sheen;
Her breasts and belly, of my vine the clusters,

Like evil angels rose, my fancy twitting,
To kill the peace which over me she'd thrown,
And to disturb her from the crystal throne
Where, calm and solitary, she was sitting.

So swerved her pelvis that, in one design,
Antiope's white rump it seemed to graft
To a boy's torso, merging fore and aft.
The talc on her brown tan seemed half-divine.

The lamp resigned its dying flame. Within,
The hearth alone lit up the darkened air,
And every time it sighed a crimson flare
It drowned in blood that amber-coloured skin.

Translated from the French by Roy Campbell

ERNEST DOWSON

Non Sum Qualis Eram Bonae Sub Regno Cynarae

Last night, ah, yesternight, betwixt her lips
    and mine
There fell thy shadow, Cynara! thy breath
    was shed
Upon my soul between the kisses and the wine;
And I was desolate and sick of an old passion,
   Yea, I was desolate and bowed my head:
I have been faithful to thee, Cynara! in
    my fashion.

All night upon mine heart I felt her warm
    heart beat,
Night-long within mine arms in love and sleep
    she lay;
Surely the kisses of her bought red mouth were sweet;
But I was desolate and sick of an old passion,
   When I awoke and found the dawn was gray:
I have been faithful to thee, Cynara! in
    my fashion.

I have forgot much, Cynara! gone with the wind,
Flung roses, roses riotously with the throng,
Dancing, to put thy pale, lost lilies out
    of mind;
But I was desolate and sick of an old passion,
  Yea, all the time, because the dance was long:
I have been faithful to thee, Cynara! in
    my fashion.

I cried for madder music and for stronger
    wine,
But when the feast is finished and the lamps
    expire,
Then falls thy shadow, Cynara! the night is thine;
And I am desolate and sick of an old passion,
  Yea, hungry for the lips of my desire:
I have been faithful to thee, Cynara! in
    my fashion.

GERALD MASSEY
O Lay Thy Hand in Mine, Dear!

O lay thy hand in mine, dear!
   We're growing old, we're growing old;
But Time hath brought no sign, dear,
   That hearts grow cold, that hearts grow cold.
'Tis long, long since our new love
   Made life divine, made life divine;
But age enricheth true love,
   Like noble wine, like noble wine.

And lay thy cheek to mine, dear,
   And take thy rest, and take thy rest;
Mine arms around thee twine, dear,
   And make thy nest, and make thy nest.
A many cares are pressing
   On this dear head, on this dear head;
But Sorrow's hands in blessing
   Are surely laid, are surely laid.

O lean thy life on mine, dear!
   'Twill shelter thee, 'twill shelter thee.
Thou wert a winsome vine, dear,
   On my young tree, on my young tree:
And so, till boughs are leafless,
   And Song-birds flown, and Song-birds flown,
We'll twine, then lay us, griefless,
   Together down, together down.

W. B. YEATS
When You Are Old

When you are old and grey and full of sleep,
And nodding by the fire, take down this book,
And slowly read, and dream of the soft look
Your eyes had once, and of their shadows deep;

How many loved your moments of glad grace,
And loved your beauty with love false or true,
But one man loved the pilgrim soul in you,
And loved the sorrows of your changing face;

And bending down beside the glowing bars,
Murmur, a little sadly, how Love fled
And paced upon the mountains overhead
And hid his face amid a crowd of stars.

ALFRED, LORD TENNYSON
June Bracken and Heather

To –

There on the top of the down,
The wild heather round me and over me June's high blue,
When I look'd at the bracken so bright and the heather so brown,
I thought to myself I would offer this book to you,
This and my love together,
To you that are seventy-seven,
With a faith as clear as the heights of the June-blue heaven,
And a fancy as summer-new
As the green of the bracken amid the gloom of the heather.

Parting

COVENTRY PATMORE
A Farewell

With all my will, but much against my heart,
We two now part.
My Very Dear,
Our solace is, the sad road lies so clear.
It needs no art,
With faint, averted feet
And many a tear,
In our opposed paths to persevere.
Go thou to East, I West.
We will not say
There's any hope, it is so far away.
But, O, my Best,
When the one darling of our widowhead,
The nursing Grief,
Is dead,
And no dews blur our eyes
To see the peach-bloom come in evening skies,
Perchance we may,
Where now this night is day,
And even through faith of still averted feet,
Making full circle of our banishment,
Amazed meet;
The bitter journey to the bourne so sweet
Seasoning the termless feast of our content
With tears of recognition never dry.

MARGARET VELEY
A Japanese Fan

Though to talk too much of Heaven
    Is not well,
Though agreeable people never
    Mention Hell,
Yet the woman who betrayed me,
    Whom I kissed,
In that bygone summer taught me
    Both exist.
I was ardent, she was always
    Wisely cool,

So my lady played the traitor –
    I, the fool.
Oh! your pardon! but remember
    If you please,
I'm translating: this is only
    Japanese.

MATTHEW ARNOLD
Isolation. To Marguerite

We were apart; yet, day by day,
I bade my heart more constant be.
I bade it keep the world away,
And grow a home for only thee;
Nor feared but thy love likewise grew,
Like mine, each day, more tried, more true.

The fault was grave! I might have known,
What far too soon, alas! I learned –
The heart can bind itself alone,
And faith may oft be unreturned.
Self-swayed our feelings ebb and swell –
Thou lov'st no more; – Farewell! Farewell!

Farewell! – and thou, thou lonely heart,
Which never yet without remorse
Even for a moment didst depart
From thy remote and spherèd course
To haunt the place where passions reign –
Back to thy solitude again!

Back! with the conscious thrill of shame
Which Luna felt, that summer-night,
Flash through her pure immortal frame,
When she forsook the starry height
To hang over Endymion's sleep
Upon the pine-grown Latmian steep.

Yet she, chaste queen, had never proved
How vain a thing is mortal love,
Wandering in Heaven, far removed.
But thou hast long had place to prove
This truth – to prove, and make thine own:
'Thou has been, shalt be, art, alone.'

Or, if not quite alone, yet they
Which touch thee are unmating things –
Ocean and clouds and night and day;
Lorn autumns and triumphant springs;
And life, and others' joy and pain,
And love, if love, of happier men.

THOMAS HARDY

In the Vaulted Way

In the vaulted way, where the passage turned
To the shadowy corner that none could see,
You paused for our parting, — plaintively:
Though overnight had come words that burned
My fond frail happiness out of me.

And then I kissed you, despite my thought
That our spell must end when reflection came
On what you had deemed me, whose one long aim
Had been to serve you; that what I sought
Lay not in a heart that could breathe such blame.

But yet I kissed you: whereon you again
As of old kissed me. Why, why was it so?
Do you cleave to me after that light-tongued blow?
If you scorned me at eventide, how love then?
The thing is dark, Dear. I do not know.

CHRISTINA ROSSETTI
Song

When I am dead, my dearest,
   Sing no sad songs for me;
Plant thou no roses at my head,
   Nor shady cypress tree:
Be the green grass above me
   With showers and dewdrops wet;
And if thou wilt, remember,
   And if thou wilt, forget.

I shall not see the shadows,
   I shall not feel the rain;
I shall not hear the nightingale
   Sing on, as if in pain;
And dreaming through the twilight
   That doth not rise nor set,
Haply I may remember,
   And haply may forget.

PHILIP BOURKE MARSTON
Inseparable

When thou and I are dead, my dear,
　The earth above us lain;
When we no more in autumn hear
　The fall of leaves and rain,
Or round the snow-enshrouded year
　The midnight winds complain;

When we no more in green mid-spring,
　Its sights and sounds may mind,—
The warm wet leaves set quivering
　With touches of the wind,
The birds at morn, and birds that sing
　When day is left behind;

When, over all, the moonlight lies,
　Intensely bright and still;
When some meandering brooklet sighs
　At parting from its hill,
And scents from voiceless gardens rise,
　The peaceful air to fill;

When we no more through summer light
   The deep dim woods discern,
Nor hear the nightingales at night,
   In vehement singing, yearn
To stars and moon, that dumb and bright,
   In nightly vigil burn;

When smiles and hopes and joys and fears
   And words that lovers say,
And sighs of love, and passionate tears
   Are lost to us, for aye –
What thing of all our love appears,
   In cold and coffined clay?

When all their kisses, sweet and close,
   Our lips shall quite forget;
When, where the day upon us rose,
   The day shall rise and set,
While we for love's sublime repose,
   Shall have not one regret,–

Oh, this true comfort is, I think,
   That, be death near or far,
When we have crossed the fatal brink,
   And found nor moon nor star,
We know now, when in death we sink,
   The lifeless things we are.

Yet one thought is, I deem, more kind,
   That when we sleep so well,
On memories that we leave behind
   When kindred souls shall dwell,
My name to thine in words they'll bind
   Of love inseparable.

EMILY BRONTË
Remembrance

Cold in the earth, and the deep snow piled above thee!
Far, far removed, cold in the dreary grave!
Have I forgot, my Only Love, to love thee,
Severed at last by Time's all-severing wave?

Now, when alone, do my thoughts no longer hover
Over the mountains, on that northern shore,
Resting their wings where heath and fern-leaves cover
Thy noble heart for ever, ever more?

Cold in the earth, and fifteen wild Decembers
From those brown hills have melted into spring:
Faithful indeed is the spirit that remembers
After such years of change and suffering!

Sweet Love of youth, forgive if I forget thee
While the World's tide is bearing me along:
Sterner desires and darker hopes beset me,
Hopes which obscure, but cannot do thee wrong!

No later light has lightened up my heaven,
No second morn has ever shone for me;
All my life's bliss from thy dear life was given,
All my life's bliss is in the grave with thee.

But when the days of golden dreams had perished
And even Despair was powerless to destroy,
Then did I learn how existence could be cherished,
Strengthened and fed without the aid of joy.

Then did I check the tears of useless passion,
Weaned my young soul from yearning after thine;
Sternly denied its burning wish to hasten
Down to that tomb already more than mine.

And even yet, I dare not let it languish,
Dare not indulge in memory's rapturous pain;
Once drinking deep of that divinest anguish,
How could I seek the empty world again?

*

Come, the wind may never again
Blow as now it blows for us;
And the stars may never again shine as now they shine;
Long before October returns,
Seas of blood will have parted us;
And you must crush the love in your heart, and I the love
    in mine!

*

If grief for grief can touch thee,
If answering woe for woe,
If any ruth can melt thee,
Come to me now!

I cannot be more lonely,
More drear I cannot be!
My worn heart throbs so wildly
'Twill break for thee.

And when the world despises,
When heaven repels my prayer,
Will not mine angel comfort?
Mine idol hear?

Yes, by the tears I've poured thee,
By all my hours of pain,
O I shall surely win thee,
Beloved, again!

Index of Poets & Poems